The Philosophy of Cash:
An Introductory Guide to Building Wealth in America Today
By D.L Edison

"The Philosophy of Cash: An Introductory Guide to Building Wealth in America Today" ©

Copyright November 2019 by D. L Edison

Published by Two Good Girls Publishing

All rights reserved. Except for the use in any review, the reproduction or utilization of this work in whole or in part in any form is prohibited without the written permission of the author.

This is a work of fiction. Names, characters, places and incidences are either the product of the author's imagination or are used fictitiously and any resemblance to actual persons, living or dead, business establishments, events or locals is entirely coincidental.

For questions and comments about this book please contact the author at; DL@DLEdison.com or check out www.DLEdison.com

Disclaimer

This book is a work of fiction. It is entirely sourced from my imagination, conjecture and hearsay. I am not a Certified Financial Planner, Stockbroker nor do I hold any licensing from the Securities Exchange Commission. I am in no way a CPA nor tax professional.

This work is not to be taken as professional advice. In my career my unprofessionalism garnered me three immediate terminations and several, "serious talks" with human resources. I am in no part an investment counselor.

For My Father, Joe
No matter where we've been in the world,
you've always been there for me.
Thank you, Dad.

Introduction

Nobody is ever going to watch your money more diligently, more closely than you. Nobody is ever going to be happier with your financial wins as you are and nobody is *ever*, *ever*, going to be more disappointed with your financial losses than you. This is the one and only financial guarantee I will assure you.

I never could understand the rationalization in giving someone else my money to manage none the less paying that individual to watch over and invest my cash. It's this idea that has always been with me in thinking of money management that exposed me to many different investment markets and it's this experience I detail in this book.

I propose we all become our own best advocate in every facet of life including creating wealth, maintaining health and defining our passions.

From a young age before I ever had a dime to invest, I seemed to have had an affinity for cash. I remember as small boys trading my older brother nickels for his quarters, him thinking they were all the same value while I was in the know. My curiosity in cash continued to grow and reached a peak when I first heard of money-making money.

While growing up I occasionally went Bass fishing with a cousin and uncle of mine. The three of us had fantastic times on the weekend jaunts we'd take, staying in a hotel, eating out, horsing around and of course fishing. I have wonderful memories of these good times.

My Uncle Tim was a commodities trader and owned a seat on The Chicago Board of Trade and it was through him, often on our weekend getaways, that I came to know what it meant to, "make a lot of money in a day," and to "lose money." Until then I couldn't conceive of how a guy could go to work one day and make X dollars and the next make XXX dollars at the very same job.

"This was the world of finance and investing," my Uncle explained. The reality of this abstract concept of dollars coming and going was felt one weekend when we had to cancel a planned fishing trip due to my Uncle, "losing a lot of money."

Upon hearing of the cancelation, I remember naively asking my cousin if we could maybe help him find his lost money, as if it were a bundle of hundreds sitting in a box in an empty lot down the street. If only it were that easy.

My cousin laughed at me, he was long aware of the highs and lows the Board of Trade elicited. And my financial education commenced. Apparently, it had been a bad week for orange juice on the exchange and even I, lowly ole eleven-year-old me, felt the squeeze. As an adult looking back, I can only imagine the staggering sums my Uncle Tim lost that week.

As the title states, this is a book of philosophy, an abstract, general idea of how to build wealth in America today. I don't offer deep specifics in terms of investment strategy, or methodology. Peter Lynch and many others have done an excellent job writing at an in-depth level, this book is a great wealth creation overview. It's very topical, very general and an excellent resource for those dipping their toe into the waters of investing for the first time.

I have broken my book into three parts: the how, the what, the why. The how details with physical action, what you can immediately do to solidify a foundation for building wealth. The what is an overview of types of investment vehicles most readily available and customary.

When I say customary it means I discuss; The US Stock Market, the US housing market, buying Bonds, precious metals and the like, NOT how to get rich fast by shorting a derivative or trading foreign currency. No matter what anybody says I maintain the Iraq Dinar is likely *not,* going to make a comeback.

I don't offer an insiders three prong approach to immediate riches. I discuss investing in sound investment fundamentals, this is what I know works

The why is simply asking you, the reader, to think of what wealth will do for you. You must set your own realistic expectations. As far as I'm concerned wealth is not, by my definition, contingent on X number of zeros – it's all about one's lifestyle.

For me, wealth is freedom from constraints such as a nine to five job. Wealth is, for me, more than anything –

time. Time to enjoy life, time to search and explore this world, time to build relationships and time to grow as an individual. Wealth, to me, means freedom, escape from convention. It means supreme independence.

I don't need a supercar, I don't need a billion dollars, I don't need an exotic animal that costs ten grand a month to support. I need time and I use money to buy time.

If I did go out and buy say a $100,000. car, which isn't much when you are talking about luxury automobiles, I would be spending two or three years that the $100,000. could buy me.

My overhead is so low these days, I could possibly stretch $100,000. to cover four years and in that time do whatever the heck I want. I do not have a single need in this world nor does my family, any wants we have are usually easily satisfied. I do not live miserly, I go out often, take vacations and weekend getaways, I eat well and live in good health.

The last hundred grand I spent went to writing my last couple of books. It also went to getting my wife an advanced degree at school, it bought us both precious time to be able to do these things.

That's not to say I can't appreciate someone working, accumulating wealth, buying expensive things like a $100,000 car. We all must decide what we want out of this world, and for me the "stuff" isn't important, but my self-exploration, discovery and time leaves me wealthy.

***

After I graduated college, I became a voracious consumer. When I started making good money I enjoyed buying "stuff." After a while, considering the people in my life, I began to see there was no depth in my world. It was entirely superficial and pretentious. In hindsight it was wretchedly stomach-turning.

The people, the careers, the empty aspirations, constant one upping each other. I needed to reassess my priorities, so I checked out for a few years, I was able to do so because of my financial position.

Unfortunately, I did not know what my passions in life were at the time, so it was not time best spent, but then the older I get the more I see there are no coincidences in life. That said I figure I needed to waste a few years to find myself. Wealth allowed me to do so.

Wealth for one reader may be a billion dollars, wealth may be a million dollars for another investor. Decide what wealth is for you, and it may be as easy as a number. Think about what you want: zeros in a bank account, a string of rental property, a chain of yoga studios, a super-hot partner that loves your money (and hopefully you too) or a supercar.

I am not a genius insider privy to market secrets, I am however absolutely convinced we all can improve our financial situation and this book outlines discernable steps to get there. What you do with the wealth you accumulate is up to you. I implore you to consider contributing something to humanity. Anything, so long as it is positive.

The How

Wealth is not a number, it's all about the lifestyle baby!

As far as I'm concerned having a net worth of a million dollars does not necessarily make me wealthy. Regardless of how much money I have in the bank if I have a big mortgage, I must work to pay every month, I'm a slave. If I have a few leased luxury vehicles that I must pay on monthly, I'm a slave. If I'm required to go to a job, even if it's high paying, that I need to sustain my lifestyle, but I'd love to skip it, I'm a slave.

I've never had a sit down with a billionaire, but I imagine chatting with Bill Gates, Jeff Bezos or Elon Musk would eventually lead to them mentioning passion as being the key motivator in building their empires, more so than the mere accumulation of zeros. Reading their bio's and following their work in the world they seem to be an incredibly passionate group of men. I trust they are motivated by helping the world, making positive contributions as much if not more than growing their institutions.

A curious thought just came to mind, I nearly forgot about the one brush I did have with a billionaire. At the time I believe he was the sixteenth richest man in the world.

I was working for an Indian National engineering conglomerate and this guy was the dead founders seventy-year old son who was the majority shareholder. I ended up in a conference room with him after he came out to the United States to tour some of the company's technical offices. Some billionaires are just zeros for the sake of zeros, completely devoid of an even a smidge of passion.

Such was the story of this fatty, monotone sloth. I watched him from across the table as he droned on about the companies worldwide offices and their profits all I could think was, "what a colossal blowhard."

He gave round the world financial news reports and blah blah blah'd until he had the others in the room ready for naptime. Personally, forget naptime, I was nearing the need to perform Seppuku.

Consistent Repetition

Consistent repetition and self-discipline are key to creating wealth as well as every success in life. Simply put the idea of consistent repetition is finding what works and then doing it again. Put five bucks aside for your investment fund then do it again on your next payday. Developing good saving habits is crucial. Methodical, steady saving becomes a good habit, manically putting aside $8 every other month or so is a bad saving habit. I hope this is obvious.

Restraint builds both character and bank accounts. And restraining from indulging in ones every want will allow a person to immediately start building wealth.

I am not a proponent of self-deprivation but of self-control. Think of this: what has five bucks ever really done for you except fill your belly with a crappy, processed fast food burger that you know you'll pay for later or a cup of overpriced coffee ten times more expensive than a K-Cup.

If you were to put away in savings a mere 5% of your net pay (what you take home after taxes and other deductions.), for each hundred dollars you make, you are only talking about five bucks. That still leaves you with $95.00 out of each hundred, the five-dollar difference is negligible, likely it'll go unnoticed.

If a person had a bi-weekly (every other week) net pay of $1,500, at a 5% saving rate they would have $75 to save twice a month. It's easy to see how forgoing a cheeseburger now and again for six months will give a fastidious saver nearly a thousand dollars of working capital. Working capital is nothing more than money that makes money. It's the total of liquid (at your immediate disposal) cash dollars you have for investing.

In our example, if the new 5% saver were to get a raise, even a small, a pathetic and insulting miniscule one, that additional income can be put, in whole or in part, into savings without having to cut back on burgers or coffee at all.

You must start somewhere to go anywhere. If you don't do it today, what makes you think you'd do it tomorrow

Plot your course not where you'd like to be when starting, start today exactly where and what you are. Begin your journey where you are today, be practical.

Be fervent in building a good, solid personal credit history. Without one, wealth will usually be out of reach. Borrowing money, working with somebody else's funds, is critical to financial success.

I mentioned earlier we must be our own best advocate, I believe this to be vastly important particularly in the workplace. If you are earning your keep and, without being greedy, you earnestly feel you deserve a raise –ask for one. If there's a senior position that you want within the organization which you work –plot a course to get it.

Be audacious. Be bold, challenge yourself. Stop worrying about your image, stop being concerned about what your co-workers might think of you. What they think of you is none of your business.

Success is as easy as making a grocery list, plot it out and make it happen. Develop good habits.

Traits of a financially successful person.

In fact, there are several traits many super-wealthy individuals possess. Many are critical to their financial success. Here is the list I compiled that includes traits, or habits, of highly successful people.

There is no order or ranking, simply a list of habits rich people have:

Exercise- This is very important for a clear mind.

Passion- Have passion in life. More on this later

Abilities- Know your strengths and weakness, harness both to your advantage.

Independence- Trust in yourself, trust your judgement. Be your own best advocate.

Actualization- Have a vision, to make it happen, visualize until it does. This is a very powerful tool. And we are exactly what we say we are.

If you tell yourself something and you fiercely believe it, and know you can do it, it's only a matter of time before your dreams materialize. If you say you are going to retire at fifty with X amount of money, visualize how to get there and you are on your way.

Invest in what you believe in and what you appreciate.

Develop patience and acceptance. Patience will allow you to better use your time. The more patience you have, the less potential stressful situations you will find yourself in thus allowing you time to focus on productive, useful endeavors. It's amazing and once you develop this habit, you'll see how much patience improves your life.

Trust in yourself and become your most reliable and honest supporter. Give yourself praise when you are successful. When you deserve it, pat yourself on the back, literally. And when they occur, acknowledge deficits and losses but do not condemn or berate yourself over them. Accept and move on. Learn and correct errors. Be fluid.

***

It's your responsibility to know the temperature of your industry and what employee demand and competitive pay is. Start plotting where you are going to get your initial investment capital. Go to the well that is already flowing. Instead of pulling out your hair trying to figure where you're going to get $500. to open a brokerage account, look to your current situation first for answers. If it's important, you'll find it.

Have an immediate financial goal. An identifiable financial target you wish to hit, it must be an appreciating asset not a sweet pair of sneakers or a trip to Las Vegas.

Appreciating assets are those whose value is anticipated to increase. Real Estate, stock certificates, bonds, Gold, these are things most of us inherently understand and agree as having a value which will likely increase.

We understand the house we buy today will cost more than it cost twenty years earlier, we can't go back in time so, being the asset (the house) appreciated in value, today it costs more.

I started building wealth initially in the stock market because, for me, it was the most easily accessible. All I needed was $500 to open a brokerage account. Before investing your hard earned and saved cash, know your trustee (the holder of your stock). Don't invest through Crazy Al's online, offshore brokerage firm. Prices are extremely competitive between brokers so there's no need to shop on the cheapest. Back to basics, have a goal to acquire an appreciating asset.

Live Below Your Means
i.e. Don't go hungry on Wednesday waitin' for your paycheck on Friday.

This is the easiest, most initially impactful, and greatest long-term habit that is applicable life-long and in every situation. It will always result in an immediate payoff. Every time. Living below your means is critical. Period.

It's the easiest thing we can do to improve our financial situation, yet it is without a doubt the single most difficult habit to develop for most of us. Every single source of media in our lives scream at us to buy this or that or proclaim they have the solution for happiness and eternal bliss for the low, low "donation," of $10.95.

Once we step out our front door, we are the target by an onslaught of consumer demanding sources. Buy what you need, treat yourself once in a while but pay attention to what and where you are spending money. Take note of your needs and cut back on the wants.

Have you ever known someone who, without fail, is perpetually broke? Who seemingly no matter how much money they're making or how soon after a payday it is, they're eternally cashless. That's a learned behavior. That learned behavior typically takes to a doctrine of blame and woe is me.

Making money is for those than can adapt to challenges, stomach risk and respect reward. A disposition of blame and dour will always be broke, while risk, willingness and curiosity will always enrich. Always.

Living below one's means isn't a single purchase or a limited, individual act, it's a lifestyle that's motivated *not* by leasing a new BMW, but by taking great satisfaction in having cash money in the bank to outright purchase two new BMW's if you wanted. But instead, you drive a seven-year old, nicely appointed Japanese automobile.

Keeping up with the Jones' or Kardashians is a futile effort.

The abundant impactful things done to live below one's means aren't conceding on big purchases like a new car, it's the multitude of small, daily decision made that greatly effect wealth.

As I mentioned, a cup of drip coffee from home versus a tall skinny mocha is money in the bank. Having a to-go cup from home even if you can easily afford the expensive mocha, is living below your means. Living below one's means is simply asking the question, "just because I can, should I?"

The concept of living below one's means should be pervasive throughout your entire life: So, you can afford a Lexus, buy a Toyota instead and live below your means. So, you can afford 3,000 sq. foot of house with a mountain view, buy the charming 1800sq ft cozy bungalow in a good neighborhood that needs a little attention and live below your means. From your coffee to your car to your home, live below your means.

This concept is not only proactive in building wealth, is also reactive in protecting what you have.

Think of this; say a business executive making $100,000 annually was in the market for a new house and she was approved for a $400,000. home loan.

If she buys at the top of her buying power, her mortgage will be contingent on her making $100,000. but what happens in the event there's a downturn in her business sector or worse, she gets laid-off?

That big old mortgage would be daunting on unemployment insurance. Had the executive purchased a home for $250,000, not only would she have been able to save the difference on her lower cost monthly mortgage, in a financial pinch it will be easier, less stressful, to afford.

***

I once worked for a brilliant Canadian telecommunication giant. There were more than a hundred thousand employees worldwide and the company had been around for a hundred and ten years. You'd think after all that time job security would be rock solid, right? Within three short years of me coming onboard the company dissolved and every single employee, worldwide, lost their job. At the time my $20,000. monthly corporate income dropped to $2,000 courtesy of state unemployment insurance.

While many of my associates went into shock and scrambled to find whatever jobs they could because they had extremely high overhead at home, I bought a season ski pass and hit the hill. I was able to do so because I lived in the same house that I did years earlier when I was only making $60,000. yearly.

I drove a five-year-old non-luxury but nice SUV vehicle which I paid cash for and I never stopped brewing coffee at home. In fact, the ski pass I bought was a low-priced mid-week pass. Even in a splurge I continually lived below my means. Besides have you been to a ski resort on a January Saturday? It's all crying snot nose kids and their up-tight, irritated mothers complaining about the long lines.

Truth be told, when this layoff occurred, I also had a gorgeous brand-new BMW M3 sports car. Like I said earlier, I'm not about self-deprivation but self-control and the BMW was very much so, a controlled, expensive indulgence. I sold the BMW as it was a, "nice to have," and not a necessity.

A sports sedan isn't particularly an investment but if you shop smart you can get a good deal that will minimize your losses when you sell. Indulging in a car or a vacation, perhaps exotic Nepalese tea pots are by all means worthy expenses.

I think we must treat ourselves, especially when we've been financially successful and worked hard for our money. We just need to be aware of how much we're spoiling ourselves. There is nothing good in being excessive. Obsessive over-consumption is never pretty.

While I ditched my car and hit the ski hill many of my ex co-workers, upon employment release, were on the hook for a long-term auto lease on very high end, very expensive luxury cars: Porsche, S Class Mercedes, Maserati.

Every executive on my team had a brand-new car one way or another, the way this came about was a year before the company's death spiral began, we all received a flat auto allowance rather than submitting mileage for reimbursement as we had been.

Now the year was 1999 and the tech bubble was still expanding its bulge and our extremely well-paid selves were each handed a six-hundred-dollar monthly car allowance. Now, that kind of money went extremely far considering the average monthly gas reimbursement was $125. maybe $150. This was a golden time in the world of account management in technology and I'll be the first to say, we were all spoiled. Big time.

The long and short of it was immediately after learning of this "found money" issued from the company, the entirety of team members bought brand new cars. It was this kind of rapaciousness that eventually broke the back of the once highly esteemed, glorious century old institution and left a hundred thousand professionals scrambling to cover whatever indulgences they incurred.

The BMW was easy for me to sell and my five-year-old truck suited me quite well that winter driving up to the ski hill to indulge in precious, carefree deliverance.

One of the greatest tragedies in this event was many of the older gentlemen I worked with had their entire retirement tied into the company's stock and lost it all. One associate had just celebrated his fifty-fourth birthday and was planning his retirement when he got his lay-off notice.

He was sure it would never come, he had been with the company since college. He deluded himself in thinking he was impervious to losing his job, not after nearly thirty years of service. He had recently purchased a new Porsche 911 too, his dream car. The day came when he received his termination notice. He committed suicide two days later.

Pay yourself first. This is the definition of dynamic saving

If you're apathetically grinding away at a forty hour a week corporate job, as about sixty-five percent of

Americans report they are, you probably looking forward to the day you retire and vacate your position. Only about fifteen percent of Americans say they really love their jobs and anticipate they'll do it as long as possible.

The other twenty percent are the truly diabolically unhappy souls, disgusted with their position in life. To the point they say they actually hate their work.

I've worked with a few of these miserable individuals over the years. It was always easy to point these twenty percent people out, they consistently complained about management, compensation, work hours, and in all their complaining I would think, "why the heck don't you go out and get another job?"

In my corporate days (I was one of the sixty-five percenter, eeh…) Many jobs I had were interesting, sometimes fun, some high paying and respectable, but none of my corporate gigs ever, ever got me as supercharged and fired up as I was five years ago publishing my first book. I would never have known what it was like to write and publish a book had I not paid myself first.

Again, when you make more money, pay yourself more. You are the one working all week so before you pay a single bill or creditor, pay yourself.

After a raise, bonus or new job with higher income than previously, pay yourself first and pay yourself more. Be it contributing to your savings or brokerage investment account or funding your IRA, make these accounts a priority over every other expense. You are worth it. Yes.

***

The last corporate job I had was that of a SDET, a software development engineer in test. I worked on a voice over IP communication platform. The work was interesting, challenging –very left brain.

Today my life is strictly right brain, creative writing, playing music, idling away the day thinking of new characters and plot twists to use, cracking myself up. I force myself to forget what it's like to diagnose a corrupt front-end server in a complex topology. I'd rather spend time thinking of the color green. Or yellow.

The one thing I retain from this former career of mine is the SCRUM model of software development. It's simply a methodology to track the life cycle of a project from beginning to end.

It breaks down, what can be a multifaceted, behemoth project, into easy bite size bits of action. Sometimes a project that seems overwhelming, starting a savings program when you're late on paying a wireless bill, for example, can be daunting. SCRUM can help you get there.

I think goals are very important. The SCRUM model helped with my goal of figuring out how to get a book written and published.

Plot out your goal from where you are right now, and where you want to be. In-between write out an action, say saving five dollars a day, that you are required to do before moving on in the "life-cycle," of you saving project.

Take responsibility for the action that is required prior to moving on in the cycle, say, cut back on one tall Vente Latte daily, which would satisfy your five-dollar goal. You could then move on to say, where you want to allocate that five-dollars.

In short, write out your wealth accumulation goal, and do it with detail. "Make a million dollars in three years," scrawled on a nasty wrinkled piece of paper jammed into the corner of your bathroom mirror won't do. It's your future after all, if this simple act is too difficult or time consuming, maybe being wealthy isn't for you. It's not for everyone, clearly. Otherwise nobody would be poor. And I wouldn't sell a single copy of this book. But I will.

***

Life has a way of hitting us in the pocketbook, seemingly for sport. Something requiring immediate attention (and money) will always come up. I will qualify this as a guarantee; something will always come up. Imagine: your dog ate a bad can of chili that you threw out deep in the trash can. Your pooch now requires immediate medical attention, attention that is going to cost you $2,500.

This example is close to the truth for a friend of mine. This guy's wife, whom he had been married to for less than six months, gave him a puppy Golden Retriever for Christmas.

Now my buddy, Paul Crawford, wasn't a dog guy. He didn't have a dog while he was growing up, in fact he never remotely expressed interest in those of a canine persuasion. So, he gets a puppy from his new bride and faked thanks and interest so not to break her heart. Six months after adopting the puppy retriever, the poor little fluffy ball of joy could barely walk. It needed either immediate hip surgery or to be euthanized.

Paul was a smart money manager, he had savings broken into several buckets (accounts), including one for emergencies. After six months he was still not sold on the idea of the dog and preferred the $150. Option of euthanasia. His wife and two kids protested profusely. He capitulated and withdrew $2,500. out of his fast access account.

Paul was ready for the unknown, knowing it is always just around the corner.

Who Do You Love?

Love is a beautiful thing, but it can be financially crippling. Finding a financially like-minded lover makes love a fiscally sound, prudent endevor. Falling in love without taking your partners fiscal temperature can be absolutely devastating.

The idea that love conquers all is wonderfully poetic but it's not incredibly practical. If your partner has poor habits when it comes to managing money and you're on a mission of wealth accumulation, it is imperative the two of you get on the same page otherwise the likelihood of reaching your monetary goals is poor at best.

If one person in a marriage is a spendthrift, while their soul mate is miserly, constantly attempting to school their partner on the benefits of saving, there will likely be discord, indefinitely …

There will always be a separation, a divide that has the potential to sever an otherwise good relationship. Money will make or break two people. If a couple can't get together on their finances, turmoil will perpetually thrive. Love may continue to exist as an undercurrent for a time perhaps but even the deepest love will drown in economic unrest.

This is a good fundamental principal outside of romantic relationships as well. If a point of contention exists between two people unless they can see eye to eye, it will remain in effect forever. Imaging it's not there is a popular "fix," eventually it will fail as will the relationship.

Consistent Repetition, Again

The summer of 2005 I went from the end of May through the beginning of September without a shower or bath. While this is accurate and indeed fact, it is not a good example of consistent repetition because, do I really need to explain? It was a real bad time and I was in a bad space.

Looking back, bathing seemed to do nothing more than complicate matters at the time and well before I knew it, I had gone three and a half months, Memorial Day to Labor Day, without my body contacting a bar of soap and warm water. I had no friends but hanger-on's around at the time and none of them appeared to be disturbed by my vociferous odor. As I said, 2005 was a really bad time for me.

Applying consistent repetition is simply finding what works for you and then doing it again. Stick with your successes. When you get used to paying yourself before your bills, you'll build confidence in your ability to save. Once you have confidence in yourself, you'll find it easy to replicate. Also, as you pour through mundane monthly expenses like the water bill, auto insurance and rent, knowing you've already been paid can ease the stress usually felt after finding what is, "leftover."

It is important to hold yourself accountable. If you outline a savings program, stick to it. Adjust it as necessary if economics mandate so, instead of discontinuing for a time, reduce your contribution if times get tight. The key again is consistent repetition. Once paying yourself becomes as important and as necessary as paying your rent, the habit should become seamless.

Give yourself timelines regarding your wealth building goals (use SCRUM perhaps) and put your goals in print. Put your reminder note on your bathroom mirror or somewhere you know you will see it regularly throughout the day. Visual reminders are quite powerful, even at a slight glance, just seeing your objective is inspirational and motivational.

The What

Sense in your head makes for dollars in your pocket.

     Once you have investment capitol accumulated the next step in wealth building is to make your money work for you. In deciding which investment vehicles will be best for you, start by weighing the risk versus reward ratio.

     Typically, the greatest returning investments have high risk values, investments with lower levels of risk have lower returns. In a nutshell this asks: how many sonic dips in a rollercoaster can you handle? Will you lose your lunch after the first descent or can you keep it together through the cyclone spins?

     IRA stands for Individual Retirement Account. Contributing to a retirement account is absolutely necessary. Again, contributing to a retirement account is absolutely necessary.

If you're working in corporate America, you'll find most major employers have fund-matching retirement accounts available to their employees. It is an absolute must, it is fundamentally imperative you contribute to a retirement account. In doing so you are putting two principles into action: consistent repetition and paying yourself first.

Week after week you will see you account steadily grow after repeated deposits, nurturing a burgeoning tidy sum all for you and your bottom line.

The way an employer sponsored and matched IRA (401k) is like this: You decide how much money you want to contribute to the fund, whatever the amount, it is then deducted pre-tax (before taxes are taken out) from your paycheck and deposited into the IRA account.

Most traditional company sponsored IRA's typically give employees a choice between several mutual funds (more on mutual funds soon) and their company stock for folks to invest in.

The real exciting part of a company sponsored IRA (401k) is in the matching. When a company offers employees matching funds, they most often require a vesting period, or length of time an employee must give employment service before their matched funds are paid out at 100%. This is typically ranging from a couple of years to five.

When an employer matches funds, for every dollar you save, they match your account with their pledged amount, usually anywhere from 25%-100%.

To break it down follow this example: Say each pay period you decide to contribute $200. to your company's IRA (401k). Your employer matches at a rate of 50%. Which means every two weeks when you're paid, your IRA contribution will total $300. $200 from you and an additional 50% or $100. from your employer. The $100. you are matched is usually cash or in your employers' stock. Either way, by simply participating in the plan, your money is earning a fantastic return.

But let's look even further at our example. You've saved diligently for an entire year, 26 pay periods. You've contributed a total of $5,200.00 and you were matched an additional $2,600 for the grand sum of $7,800. Hypothetically, you chose to invest your entire account in your employer's public stock, and it had a banner year increasing a whopping 20%.

After a year, you no longer feel the sting you did when you began funding your IRA and your repetitive consistency netted you approximately $9,000.

Now, matches are usually capped at about 6% meaning you'll only be able to take advantage of the extra 50% contribution from your employer for the first six percent of your annual salary. If you earned $100,000. per year and your employer matched 50% up to 6%, they would cap out at $3,000.

Sounds like a fantastic deal but the reality is less than 35% of eligible employees exercise their right to make this easy money. Nearly two thirds of Americans are passing on the opportunity to pay themselves with free money! Do not let a company sponsored retirement savings account pass you by without contributing. Do not let free money pass you by, you must contribute.

If you are working for an employer that does not offer a sponsored IRA (401k), there are other options. I love me some ROTH IRA.

Almost everyone can open and contribute to a ROTH account. Prohibitions to opening a ROTH account include making too much money and other issues that would not affect most Americans.

One of the biggest differences between the ROTH vs traditional (401k) retirement account is the traditional account is funded with pre-tax dollars, before tax is withheld, while the ROTH is funded with post-tax money, dollars which tax was already paid. The importance of this key difference is noted upon withdrawal from the retirement account.

Once an individual is eligible to withdraw money from the retirement account, they would be required to pay tax on a traditional account while taking funds out of a ROTH account, being that the money used to contribute to your ROTH, you paid tax on before you invested money, the entire balance of the account is yours, all yours

There are fees of course if one would withdraw from a retirement account prior to reaching retirement age as set by federal government typically 59 1/2. Even if you have a corporate sponsored retirement from your employer you could and should, still open a ROTH account.

***

Again, key difference between a traditional IRA and a ROTH account is the tax ramifications. A traditional IRA/401k is funded with pre-tax dollars. A Roth account is funded with post-tax dollars. When you are ready to access the money in your traditional IRA you will be required to pay tax on the money you withdraw.

As I mentioned, when you withdraw funds from your ROTH account the entire balance is tax free. Of course, there are age requirements for withdrawing, usually 59 ½, and if you access the cash before the determined age, you'd have to pay penalties for an early withdraw. Same if you access funds in a traditional IRA.

One last mention of praise regarding a Roth Account, you may withdraw your principal contributions at anytime without tax ramifications. I say this very generally and there are likely exceptions, but I have accessed Roth funds without tax consequences in the past during tight times. I believe it still to be the case (check with your tax person) an individual can draw from their Roth account without triggering taxes so long as only the original principal that was contributed, is tapped. This really means a Roth IRA can be an emergency cash account in time of need, like during the Covid-19 Outbreak.

In a pinch you can accesses your retirement money early but there would likely be a penalty to do so. Early withdraw penalties can be quite steep so be aware of the rules in whatever retirement account you open. And once again I say, it is imperative to open and fund a retirement account even if you've never done so and you are long into your career. It's not too late so long as you are eligible.

***

I love the stock market and I've learned to be a savvy investor. Between 2008 and 2015 I earned 30% annually on my stock portfolio. The basic fundamental I followed are easy to duplicate. Buy what you like, buy what you know and buy what you use.

I guess the influence my big money Uncle Tim had on me ignited my love for the Stock Market. Newcomers to investing sometimes feel overwhelmed and intimidated by the stock exchange. Like most things in life, it's as big and scary or as tame as you make it. And, again like life itself, the market is fluid, don't be fooled by linear charts.

Tameness can turn cruel in a heartbeat and vice versa.

Back in the day, full-service brokerage firms were packed to the brim with solid oak desks, recent college grads, the smell of entitled, self-serving ambition and skewed morals. These old firms made millions and the brokers that worked for the firms made millions. Every year fortunes were made from commissions, one stock trade at a time.

And these fortunes were made, built on the misconception, that trading in the stock market was extremely complex, near other worldly and it was best left for the financial geniuses in the world.

I read a report long time ago and the summary was that a monkey can throw darts at a list of stocks and pick as many winners as a trained professional. Two things, markets have averages and that monkey should have tried out for the Yankee's with the arm it had.

When it comes to investing in the stock market (i.e., picking stocks) the primary fundamental I rely on is the idea of picking, or investing in, companies I like and use. It's a rather simple strategy that has earned me 30% average annual returns.

The big ones are easy, if I'm interested in adding a technology stock to my portfolio for a long-term hold, I'll look at the devices I use at home and work, I'll then choose which manufacture I think has the best products, and the brightest future for growth and bam! There's my pick. I can't tell you the last time I factored a stock's P/E Ratio into my buying decision.

Stock certificates are traded on a stock exchange. An exchange is like a shopping mall. In a mall there are several stores. The NASDAQ trades some stocks (i.e. a mall with certain stores) whereas the New York Stock Exchange trades other stock (i.e. it's another shopping mall with entirely different stores/stock). Stock is only traded in one exchange.

Be aware of your environment, know what's going on around you. In doing so you may come across interesting investment opportunities you hadn't thought of.

If you are privy to pre-sale major IPO's, clearly you do not need to be reading this introductory guide to investing. For everyone else, IPO's (initial public offering) can be a good investment, they can be a bad investment, it all depends on the fundamentals of the company. Forget about the buzz word: IPO.

IPO simply means the stock is publicly available for purchase for the first time. Think of it like buying a new car. Depending on the manufacture and model, the car may be a great buy holding its value for years to come or even appreciating in value, becoming a prized collectable.

Or, it may depreciate 20% once you drive it off the lot, like most cars. The buzz around IPO's is generated because it is new. Like a newborn baby, everyone is delighted and interested because it is new. But we all know there are some ugly babies in the world.

When Picking Stocks Consider Your Source, Make Your Awareness Payoff

Two recent additions to my stock portfolio came about because I was fully aware of my environment. Stock number one was easy. The day I went into a Fred Meyer Grocery and saw a, "Star Wars," sticker on Dominican grown bunch of organic bananas, I knew I had to buy Dis/Disney.

I mean when a monster corporation like Disney finds a way to advertise on a widely consumed, natural, organic object I knew I was on to something. Clearly

Disney was on to something too because I'm up 35% on my money in an eleven-month window.

This coming from the only person left in America that has never seen the movie, "The Lion King." Talk about thinking out of the box, Disney hit a grand slam on the banana idea. Genius.

The second stock I bought, purely based on being aware of my surroundings, was Dominoes Pizza. One evening a while back my wife and I were in search of some hot fresh pizza and she suggested Dominoes.

When I was in college, I would often eat pizza, as was the wont of most students. It was cheap and easy. Dominoes was my mainstay. The pizza was not terribly tasty but it was always filling. Again, it was cheap and easy. After graduation I pulled away from eating budget pizza to expanding my gastric horizons on more gourmet propositions.

So, when my wife proposed grabbing a pie from this particular restaurant, I laughed at the idea. I regaled my wife with stories of cheap za by the slice while I was in college. Being in the know, she explained the chain was much improved from twenty tears prior. I conceded to the pie.

I was amazed with the improvements the corporation had made. It was obvious they were on a mission to kick up their game. The improved quality of the pie, the cheerful customer service, the bright and clean restaurant were all welcome surprises. They made an impression.

Several months later I noticed a brand-new building being constructed for this chain, no longer take-out only, this new facility had a large dining room, modern glass profile, a drive-thru window. It looked a world apart from the dingy, unkempt storefront I patronized in school.

The second time we ordered a delicious pizza from the joint I really took notice and decided to investigate the company as a potential investment. I typically stick to the technology business sector as this is what I know best, but I could not dismiss the lingering taste of perfectly cured peperoni coupled with a sensation blend of wonderful cheesy goodness.

I bought some shares of the company and caught it on its way up, before the rest of the country realized the pie maker was revamping its formula for the better.

I didn't keep the Dominoes Pizza stock very long, I had an Idea that I would watch it and shoot for a 20% return. I amiably overshot my goal and within nine months I was up 40% on my money.

Some companies I hold for years, I've had some for decades. Some, as in this case, I keep until I hit a pre-determined profit… or loss.

Let me be perfectly clear on one thing when it comes to the stock market, day trading is NOT investing. From my experience, day trading stock is dependent in two things; emotion and momentum.

Neither which have a place in investment strategy. When you place a trade because you are watching the market and you witness a shift in momentum, you are already too late to make real big money. Big money initiates momentum, it does not trail momentum. And day traders trade for big money.

You may have heard of somebody someone you know, knows, whom have made fast, fat cash by day trading stocks. In its rudimentary form, day trading is simply buying stock in a company one day and selling it the very same day.

I have bought and sold stock in the same day, but I never considered myself a day trader. I found the risk to be too much to substantiate the reward. And the anxiety that day trading caused is enough to give me a heart attack, a panic attack at the very least.

I've never met a day trader that thought 3% earnings on investment is a great day. They only look at high flying returns of 30-50% in a day. 3% is an excellent return, particularly in one day. Build your own framework. Where there is a high, there is a low in waiting. It's the nature of the market. My frame work tells me 3% is a good day because I can easily tolerate a 3% loss.

If I saw a 50% daily return, the nature of the market tells me I can anticipate a 50% loss on my investment, in a day. That's a real doozy, taking a 50% hit on your investment. That's a heavy drinking loss, that's a go home and kick your puppy cuz you're mad loss.

I don't need losses like that besides I'd never kick a puppy and I don't know that my liver could handle the extra drinking. Wild ranges from stratospheric highs to deep sea trench lows can be easily seen in the release of last years Canadian Cannabis stocks. Several saw 100%, 200% even 400% returns in a matter of months, then came the lows.

When a stock sees a 50% daily return without there being a new product release, government approval for a product, news of being bought out or some substantial reason for such high return, it's all smoke and mirrors. Or more appropriately, its momentum and emotion and absolutely zero substance.

There is wisdom in the adage, slow and steady wins the race. If you indulge in the promise of huge daily returns while day trading beware, you will be hit.

Don't ever buy a stock that you must buy today. Again, don't ever buy a stock that you must buy today.

As you move through your investment career, on occasion you may get unsolicited investment advice or as it's come to be known: *The blistering hot stock tip*. Do your due diligence.

I'm going to make one more exceptionally general, wide sweeping statement regarding investments –nothing good ever happens off-shore. Nearly every financial scam that hits the news seems to be predicated on being "off-shore." I don't recall one having had occurred "on-shore."

I wonder if the people that get caught in these scams understand what exactly "off-shore," means. I think not. Vagueness is part of the scam. If you don't understand how an investment works, why buy it.

If you don't understand how a company makes money or how their product or service works, it may not be a good investment for you. If the company itself is vague and you don't understand what they do, it may not be a good investment for you.

If someone is blaring at you, telling you about a stock that's going to make a killing soon, remember this: misery loves company. And there's no more misery than lost money misery. Okay, well life can and likely will disperse things worse than a few lost shekels.

***

I remember an elevator ride I took years ago with a few office associates back when I was a drone in corporate America. I was a mid-level manager at an old Baby Bell telecommunications company, I was working on seventh avenue in Seattle.

It was the late nineteen-nineties, organizations were vying to buy the high-speed data transport lines we were selling, the dot com bubble wasn't quite yet on the horizon and the internet market was all the rage.

It really was a bit of a gold rush, whoever had the biggest data pipe (i.e.: chunk of gold) was king and could squash or buy up the competition. Now decades later there isn't much competition, just oligarchies as big as the Amazon.

I walked into the lobby of the building from the street as I usually commuted to work via Metro, when I saw the elevator doors open, I recognized a couple of guys from my office, Kenny Cho and Bob Carter. Both good guys, solid sales execs.

We all had come on board within a year of the other and got to know each other well over the years. One of our favorite topics to shoot the breeze over was our favorite stock picks of the moment.

We were young, adventurous and single, making money hand over fist allowing for each of us an ample amount of disposable income for such necessities as fine Arturo Fuente Hemingway cigars, BMW's and poorly chosen stock picks.

We worked on the thirty-third floor so there was plenty of time, starting from the lobby, to concoct an ill-conceived plan on the way up.

Kenny Cho was one of the most compelling sales guys I ever met. He had this thing about talking with his hand that without fail could draw anyone in. He'd start out talking with a random gesture here and there, maybe touch his chin for example, but then he'd begin waving his hands wildly and they become hypnotic, like a conductor's wand. They would suck anyone in.

By the time I stepped in, Kenny's hands were already in flight, spinning a wild web, drawing Bob Carter into his spell. His fingered minuets were useless to resist. He was an incredibly sincere person too. Between his impassioned tone and magical paws, he was quite a convincing character.

I came to find Kenny was singing praises for a new company whose stock he recently acquired. Now, at the time I wasn't a big stickler on certain things I needed to research before buying a stock but, at the very least, I would do some due diligence.

On this occasion for some reason between floors twelve and twenty-nine I, without giving it a second thought, verbally committed to invest $2,500, in a company, I not only didn't know a thing about, the guy recommending it didn't know a thing about it either other than his brother-in-law said it was a good buy.

I only remembered the stock symbol, that and the fact the company was an offshore, online gambling site and it was going to make a killing due to being beyond federal regulators.

Being the height of the dot com boom, essentially any company that operated "online" was a guaranteed success. Temporarily at least. The company Kenny Cho touted as supreme folded within six months. Looking back, I can only imagine some guys in a boiler room in New Jersey laughing at us all the way to the bank.

***

Some of the fundamentals I look at while reviewing a stock include: company management including the board of directors, market cap, market share, product line and competition. This is all high level, a ten-thousand-foot overview if you will.

I don't need to know the name of every board member, but I note those I recognize, and read brief bios of key players. The market cap of a company is the total value of the organization. This is simply calculated by multiplying the stock price by the total number of outstanding company shares.

A stock's market share is the amount of business (based on dollars earned) a company has in their market segment.

For example, if a company manufactures wooden blocks, their market share is the amount of money they made in comparison to all wooden blocks sold. If the wooden block business i.e. the market segment, was booming and in totaling all the money made by all the wood block makers in America it made 50 million. If the company we invest in earned 10 million dollars, it would have a 20% market share. The more the market share the better. In capitalism, dominance is sublime.

Dividends are bonuses paid to shareholders determined by the prosperity of the company's year. Not all companies offer dividends and the amount can fluctuate vastly.

A company may pay dividends one year and not the next. These bonuses can be paid directly in cash to shareholders, more often it is used to buy more shares in the company issuing the bonus.

If you buy 20 shares in a company and after a healthy year you see a balance of 20.13 shares on your statement, it's because of the dividends paid. Dividends are a good thing.

A company's product line is self-descriptive. I buy what I like, I buy what I use. I buy what I understand. There is good money to be made in easy to understand market segments. Many people have gotten rich off of Americans love of soda pop. Family dynasties have been built on action figures.

If you use a mobile device or tablet that you really like, look at buying into the company. If you're wild about your new shampoo and you know all your friends are using it too, look at buying into the company.

If you buy gasoline at a particular gas station because you appreciate their environmental awareness and social consciousness, look at owning a piece of the company.

If you continually make changes erratically only because you have an option alternate to your current state, you may not have thought through your initial course. Think through decisions and take rational action. As much as you can, remove emotion, re-introduce it after the act. There will be time. When re-analysis of your opinion truly is required, based on fact rather than emotion, have a plan.

Don't let emotional bias conquer your rational thought. Doing so will eternally compromise your position.

When I take a negative hit on a position, I follow specific steps in re-evaluating the stock. I'll first pull back on any immediate action such as an impulsive sell and take a close look to understand the downturn. I'll figure out why it occurred.

Secondly, I'll evaluate my initial directive on the purchase, what was my intent on initially buying. I'll proceed and likely "dollar-cost average" down my position. Essentially, I'll dig in for the long haul. To dollar-cost average down on a position means to lower the average cost of a share of stock.

If I bought one share of stock in a company for $20. and the stock took a dip down to $10. per share and I bought another single share, my average cost for the two shares would be $15. If I'm confident in a stock/company dollar-costing down on a dip is a must. This is usually my case otherwise I didn't do enough due diligence and research prior to buying in the first place.

There are times to cut losses of course, be prepared by reviewing your initial target price and acceptable losses you were willing to take

In this case it's easy to get emotionally sucked into "hoping," your stock pick will miraculously gain upward momentum, but you must stick to logic. Maintain your awareness. Indulge in emotion after you make a sound financial decision.

Opportunity is Everywhere

Sometimes picking a wining stock is as easy as paying attention to what's immediately in front of you. Say you and your spouse were having a lovely dinner with your in-laws, celebrating a new home they recently acquired.

After cajoling each other with anecdotal relocating stories over a couple of bottles of wine, you find you must make your way to the lavatory at which time you ask, "say folks, point me in the direction of the restroom would yous please."

"Just down the hall dear," you enchanting mother in-law directs with implicit charm.

After finding your way to the loo and taking care of business, you flush the toilet only to find to your horror, the toilet keeps running, and running. Your mind goes into overdrive as you recall entering the tiny washroom, you realize the toilet was silent, not the least bit running when you came in. You freak out thinking you somehow busted the bowl.

Immediately you're calculating the cost of a plumber at eight P.M. on a Sunday night, more worrisome, you've got to break it to yer ex-Marine Corps Drill Instructor father in-law, ya broke his new bathroom.

"I hope he knows to jiggle the handle," your wonderful mother in-law delights as she puts out her famous cherry cobbler for dessert.

"Yeah, he probably thinks he broke it!" the old Marine chuckles.

Sometimes life is just that easy, all ya gotta do is jiggle it a little bit and it falls into place.

***

Successful investing in the stock market is not rocket science, a wonderful opportunity can be as easy as a good slice of pizza pie. One key component to successful investing is to maintain awareness. Be vigilant on understanding your environment, knowing what's going on around you is invaluable information. Knowledge is power and it will enrich any and all who take the time to absorb their environment.

With regard to the short-term hold strategy I employed in the pizza restaurant example, here are the three types of investment buckets I use: long-term hold, active trade and testing the water.

Long-term wealth is bucket number one. My long-term positions are primarily in my retirement account. These stocks are my golden geese, they keep giving year after year, providing solid respectable returns, most offering nice dividends as well.

I check the stock price for these holdings from time to time and make a trade a few times throughout the year, but these positions are happy fat sows that need minimal maintenance.

The next is the bucket of active trade positions I hold. This pool of stocks are ones that I watch regularly, maybe a couple times a day and I keep my ears perked to the news. I may trade this bucket of stocks throughout the year depending on their performance of course.

And lastly, and the absolute smallest bucket in my mix, is testing the market. I'm not much of a gambler anymore, but if I'm feeling the need for a roller coaster ride, I'll buy a few shares of something that I find appealing.

The last stock I added to my current portfolio that fell into this category was a Canadian Retail Cannabis company traded on the pink sheets. I'm a proponent for progressive change in the world so this market segment interested me. Besides watching the big swings that were happening looked like fun. I invested a little bit of money, real short term.

The pink sheets are stocks/companies traded that in a nutshell are smaller, newer and obscure compared to stocks on the major exchanges. They are not traded on a major exchange like the NASDAQ or NY Stock Exchange. They typically trade at under a few dollars or even a few cents thus they are sometimes referred to as penny stocks. Also, they don't report company financials like their counter parts on the NYSE and NASDAQ.

There are stocks that were one-time American power house companies that end up on the Pink Sheets. If a stock trading on the NYSE falls below a certain dollar amount it will be delisted. If this happens, that company could then go to the pink sheets to trade.

US tax code favors long term investing. The difference between holding a position for a few months and a year or longer is significant.

The numbers that come to mind are telling me, tax liability on short term (those held less than twelve months) securities profits are 3 times that of a long-term (more than twelve months) hold. I am not a tax guy. Hell, I'm not an investment guy. I'm a poetry writing, guitar playing fiction novelist that made good money in the US investment markets. That's all.

At the end of the year we all need to need to pony-up to Uncle Sam, it's all profit anyway so take your lumps and step aside for the next non-voluntary contributor.

Seriously, somebody must pay for the greatest country in the world.

***

Brace yourself for losses, sooner or later they will arrive at every active investor's door. Don't get emotional over losses, it's just business. The best thing you can do about losses in the stock market is to set your tolerance level.

Setting your tolerance level regarding losses is critical to one's sanity. There are many different order types other than buy sell orders.

A stop-loss order is worth being familiar with. It's as simple as it sounds, it's an order one would place to sell securities in order to minimize losses if it hits a certain low point. To stop a loss. Think of it like a security blanket, an insurance policy or a condom, all for your protection

Once a stop-loss order is placed it gives you peace of mind that if a stock price dips below a certain threshold, it would be automatically sold. This saves you from frantically scrambling for your tablet upon waking, panicking while checking prices to see if you need to sell.

Here is an example: I buy a stock at a cost of $50 per share. I have confidence in the company I bought however, I'm somewhat new to the market segment and there are government sanctions coming down the pike that have the potential to wildly effect the share price. I think the sanctions will have a positive influence, increasing the $50. share price.

Yet, there are always unknowns and I want to hedge my bet. I decide my loss tolerance level on this individual stock to be 20%. I decide I can stomach a 20% loss on my $50. stock so I put a stop loss order in. If the price falls below $40. a share the stock would be automatically sold.

I can then decide to take a carefree three-month sabbatical to the jungle of S.E. Asia in order to commune with and care for baby elephants. Without access to the internet I'd have no idea how the market is performing, nor would I know how my new stock is faring.

With my stop loss order in place I can coo to and sooth young pachyderms to my heart's content stress free knowing worst case scenario I'll be down $10 a share on said stock. You must decide what your comfort levels are. And stick to them otherwise you will always be chasing your own ghost.

Bonds are financial instruments that are essentially loans, typically issued by local or federal governments or corporations. There're used to raise capital with a promise of a guaranteed re-payment.

They are low risk, low reward. Bonds are different than a stock because bonds have a set maturity date and offer a set guaranteed rate of interest. Bonds are like IOU's and are less volatile than stocks. However, the guaranteed interest on bonds are typically quite low.

For a portfolio requiring possible access to cash in the near term, say if you're saving for a house, a rental house or some other investment, bonds are a safe refuge for your money.

Mutual Funds are essentially a pooling of many company's stock that are managed and traded as a single unit. Funds have management fees, watch for this.

For example: an imaginary mutual fund called the, "Fun Fund," has stock ownership in: an alcoholic beverage distiller, a cruise line, a theme park and a whoopie cushion manufacturer. All companies that focus on fun.

A mutual fund can be a good idea for someone who in interested in investing in a single market segment or someone who may want to invest in high tech companies that have skyscraper high price tags.

Instead of waiting to save $5,000. for five shares of a $1,000. per share company, which is common in technology, you could buy shares in a mutual fund. Mutual funds allow you to inherently minimize risk because you have many eggs in many baskets instead of ownership in one single organization.

Precious metals can be a solid investment. One drawback is gold and silver are heavy and can take up a lot of space.

Investing in gold and silver mining companies will leave more room in your safe deposit box or stash place at home and will leave you less worrisome about someone stealing your treasured bullion and keep you in the precious metals game.

Never let anyone hold or store your precious metals. If you are going to buy gold or silver, platinum bullion perhaps, you must always maintain physical control. Not doing so exposes you to great peril.

Think of this: you have $30,000. worth of American Gold Eagle rounds and they're sitting in some small business' vault on the other side of the country. For years every other paycheck you've sent this small business money to buy gold. You get a monthly statement that reflects your mushrooming balance as you add funds and the price of gold rises. Then all of a sudden, this small business declares bankruptcy and your thirty-grand worth of gold gets tied up in court. Maybe you'll see some of it, maybe not. When investing in precious metals always maintain physical control.

***

Real Estate can offer a massive ROI (return on investment). When investing in real estate most Americans will start by purchasing a single-family home. Some will buy additional single-family homes to rent out while still the smallest yet most adventurous group will buy real estate as investments in the form of multi-family units, commercial property even raw land for development.

I have experience with buying and selling single family homes, so I'll focus on this.

I have found the single biggest way to materialize huge returns in a fairly short span of time, with a relatively small investment to be flipping a single-family home.

I'm not talking about buying a dilapidated charnel house to fix up and sell as fast as possible, I'm talking about buying a nice, clean affordable house to live in and improve while banking big-league asset appreciation.

Profits are nothing until they are realized. If your 250k home appreciates 100K over a few years you may feel as though you have made a killing. In truth, you have nothing until you sell.

This is true for all investments. Unless you are willing to liquidate, the profits you are realizing are not really realized, they are an illusion, they are only potential profits. Profits are only realized when you sell.

I think of my former colleagues at the telecom giant, thinking they were set for life as our company stock hit $100 a share. By the time any of them were able to sell, the stock fluttered at $3. Until they sold, the price was only smoke and mirrors. Period.

My real estate business model calls for using the absolute least amount of money possible, to buy a home. A 20% down payment is antiquated. 3% is where the money is to be made. Going back to the importance of building great credit; the higher the FICO score, the lower the cost of borrowed money.

Buying a Home 101

Let's look at an overview comparing two real estate investment strategy. Buyer 1 is completing their transaction with a 20% down payment while buyer 2 is closing with 3% down on their property. To keep things simple, we'll say each buyer is closing on a house valued at $200,000.

Buyer 1 is closing on his property with a traditional conventional loan and $40,000 down payment. Buyer 2 is completing their purchase with a FHA loan, putting $6,000 down leaving them $34,000 to invest elsewhere.

The primary difference is FHA loans requires Private Mortgage Insurance. This usually ranges from about ½ to 1% of the purchase price. So, with our example buyer two will have to carry about $200. monthly of insurance with their loan, remember, 1% is on the high side of estimating PMI.

In ballparking financial estimates always bank on the high side of things, in doing so you'll always be pleased with the results of reality.

If buyer 2 lived in their home for five years, and they bought in a healthy real estate market, like Seattle metro, it would not be unheard of to see a property valuation increase 40-50%.

At a 40% value increase their property would now be worth $280,000. This would give buyer 2 $80,000 profit. Minus their 3% down of $6,000, they'd have $74,000 profit. Consider the $200. monthly private mortgage insurance buyer 2 paid over 60 months for a total of $12,000. Deduction the 12K from buyer 2's 74,000 profit and their total bottom line on the deal would be $62,000. Quite a considerable sum.

We'll say buyer 1 had an identical increase of their property value. They too saw an $80,000 profit upon selling after five years. However, with a 20% down, their net would be $40,000.

The difference between the two loan types is significant. Upon selling, buyer 2 ended up about 50% more net profit on their sale than buyer 1. Another notable difference over the course of 5 years is that buyer 2 had $34,000 to invest in other avenues due to their low-down payment. $34,000 invested over 5 years could see monumental return.

Also, key to consider is a property owner can refinance their mortgage loan. It used to be that a homeowner carrying an FHA loan could simply drop the required PMI upon reaching the point of having 20% equity in their property. Either by way of property value increase or by paydown of loan over time. Or a combination of the two; property value increase and monthly payments over time. I believe this is no longer the case however refinancing is an option.

Re-financing is replacing an existing loan such as your original home loan, with a new loan. This is done for a variety of reasons with the overriding motivator to do so being when interest rates go down. Swapping your FHA loan for a conventional loan after you've built equity in your property, will allow you to terminate private mortgage insurance.

And if you were able to reduce your monthly mortgage payment by no longer having to pay PMI, you should keep your monthly house payment the exact same and move the dollars you were paying for PMI, to your principal and interest.

Paying an extra hundred dollars or so toward your principal (the P in P&I) when you can will reduce the term of your loan dramatically. Years can be reduced from the term of your loan by making, even small, additional monthly payments to your loan. Doing so is paying yourself first and living below your means –in action.

When interest rates go down you can re-fi for a better rate. In addition, you can re-fi for a lower term i.e., 30 year fixed to a 15-year fixed.

In real estate one can buy into what are called, Real Estate Investment Trusts, or simply, RIT's. Investing into a RIT will allow you entry into a real estate market without going through purchasing and maintaining, individual homes.

I have never had a keen interest in being a landlord, people can be difficult and flakey.

Mortgage requirements are stiffer for rental or commercial property as compared to residential loans. The standout difference is the required down payment.

The standard down for a rental property is around 30%. Vs the low 3% on residential.

Whether the property is a residential home for you and your family, a second home to rent out or a commercial unit, a great location is crucial. Knowing your surroundings and being familiar with your geographic area is paramount in a successful real estate investment. The old adage; location, location, location, is still relevant and an absolute must today.

Buy as much house as you can comfortably (below your means) afford but stick to living below your means. Don't get the maximum loan you qualify for, get what's comfortably below your means.

Buy the odd house on a block of well-appointed homes with lovely lawns. Buy a house that needs some elbow grease but not one that is in ruins and needs to be torn down.

When deciding on a house, particularly when it's your first real estate investment, paint yourself a realistic picture on how much work you want to do to get the place to your liking. Contracting out home improvement projects is very expensive, one area a homeowner can build equity at their pace is by doing improvements themselves.

Spend a considerable amount of time in the area you are thinking of buying in. Don't rely on glossy "home for sale" magazines or even good online real estate sites. You must look at the property and neighborhood they are in. With the right-angle a good photographer can make a shanty shack look good.

What makes a good R/E buy for you will be what your buyers look for when it comes time for you to sell. Again, location, location, location. Whether you're looking for property that you will live in, a single-family home to rent or another type of property, buy quality.

School districts are very important, bus line access, convenient grocery stores and gas stations, ease to get to major freeways. These are all things likely to be assets but not listed on a property record.

I think a great house for both making a home and excellent investment would look like the following:

Lovely little place needs cosmetic work, landscaping and a fence.

As a matter of fact, a couple of months ago a sweet little old lady a few doors down from me sold her house. Her house was a buyer's dream, obviously because she had multiple offers on it within the first twenty-four hours of listing the place.

She got her full asking price, which was, of a recent flurry of four sales, the most expensive listing on our block. Plus, she got 5% over the asking.

I think her place was a great buy because it was painted pink, decades of sun bleached the façade to more of a muted salmon color. The roof, unpatched and sturdy, is like the pink paint, decades old but otherwise in good shape.

The bathroom was straight out of the 1970's. No tile was cracked, no chips in the porcelain, there were no stains on the sink or tub. It's as if the entire room was hermetically sealed then placed is a massive vault for the past forty-seven years.

The kitchen was the same way, everything was outdated; appliances, wallpaper, color, the linoleum flooring… But it was all in spectacular condition. There wasn't a dent or scuff, a nick or chip anywhere to be seen.

The entire house, garage and lawn was outdated but the condition of the place was undeniably stupendous. Incredible.

At the end of the day the neighbor's house was a good buy because it structurally sound, in a great neighborhood simply needing someone to update the house to make it a shining star on the block. The sale price reflected the need for a little work and updating but all in all, it was a steal.

I've looked at many, many homes for sale and bought several, at the end of the day what I can say is, buy below the market, understand the work ahead of you and lastly, buy what is universally pleasing, i.e.: location, location, location.

Spread your money, remember the old saying, "don't put all your eggs in one basket." Diversity is the name of the game. Diversity, with reference to investing, simply means to spread your wealth across many different markets.

The consensus of professional market makers and market raiders is to allocate your investment money in a variety of ways. Diversity brings balance to every situation.

The Why

Money for the sake of money is an absolute, pathetic empty endeavor. Money is a means to an end nothing more –Full-Stop.

Now my previous statement may incite Brueghelian pandemonium particularly in the pop culture set, those transfixed on every step that the Kardashian's make, but it's true. Money will not make you: happy, witty, more interesting or charmingly insightful. Money will make you rich. That's it. No more, no less.

You may be able to buy "friends" and cosmetically improve your appearance perhaps but give it ten years and you'd see the lift would go flat and the "friends," well they never really were. Wealth affords one the ability to buy stuff, to collect stuff, to buy better and better stuff, exotic stuff, all kinds of stuff.

I myself, young and foolish, absolutely indulged in the pursuit of stuff. I had a lot of stuff, a whole big house with seven televisions, a couple new cars and all kinds of other neat stuff. I maintained this path for quite some time until I came to the alarming conclusion; I was not at all a happy person.

Wealth in and of itself is not to be demonized, it's not a bad thing, it is simply buying power. I wasn't unhappy because I had money, I would have been just as miserable had I been penniless. At the time in my life to which I'm referencing, between the two states, rich and poor, I suppose it was better to be a party pooper and rich.

Only problem is misery loves company and being wealthy affords one to employ a cornucopia of bad company with bad intentions and bad habits.

For me, when I was young, vulnerable and passionless, I was audacious in my wealthy despair. There was nothing I could do to get out of my self-imposed, vile life. It got quite ugly.

It took a lot of time, introspection, maturity, willingness and self-resolve to find true happiness. When I knew I found my absolute passion in life, true happiness came hand-in-hand.

My greatest passion in this life is writing contemporary fiction. Unfortunately, the cosmic literary joke is: nobody reads anymore. Okay, that is a very wide, sweeping, overgeneralization of American's proclivity to pass on picking up a contemporary work of fiction but in a nutshell it's true nobody ready anymore.

I came across an interesting statistic recently that I emphatically thought to be inaccurate. Deep digging into the matter confirmed the initial claim I read stating fewer than twenty percent of adult American college grads will pick up a novel post-graduation.

Sometimes I feel like the last guy operating a blacksmith shop. Like some dude in the early 1950's, blind to the inevitable fact, hoping the automobile was just a fad and shoeing horses was on the verge of a great big comeback.

I'm stuck in my ways too, for example one of the fastest growing segments in the literary world is audio books and I will never, ever publish a novel of mine in an audio book. Full-Fu*king-Stop.

As far as I'm concerned books are meant to be read not listened to. When I read a book, I study the words the author used for conveyance, there's cadence and tone in a good book, I find rhythm to be seen and felt in the pages of a good book. This experience is lost with listening, it can only be found in seeing, through reading.

When I read Jack London, I feel like I'm getting to know the man as an individual, it's more than reading a good story. When I read a good book, I feel like I've had a conversation with the writer, like I have insight into their personality. As far as I'm concerned, audio books are for those not willing to fully commit.

Just because something isn't right for you, doesn't make it wrong for me.

The best thing money can do for you is not about stuff, as I said it's a means to an end and the end for all of us, the best thing money can do, I firmly believe, is allow one to pursue true passion in life. Finding passion in one's life fills all cracks of self-doubt, it solidifies one's direction in this physical plane, and passion creates contagious joy. Passion embodies happiness.

All the wealth in the world, without fulfilling passion in one's life, will lead to a disappointing life.

A few years ago, I read the story of a Norwegian Prince Billionaire. This guy was royalty, seriously wealthy and he was a hopeless crackhead-junkie. Someone in this man's family invented the envelope or something, affording him more money than mere mortals can imagine.

I thought about what it would be like to have an incredible, raging addiction to cocaine and heroin, and how awesome a life this guy could have had.

I mean think about it; your world is focused on a couple of mind-bending chemicals, you're absolutely hopelessly possessed by them and you have all the money in the world to procure as much as your monkey wants to consume. It would seem this behavior had to be driven by passion as well as chemical dependency.

Imagine a fortified house containing several chest high safes, each stockpiled with kilos of Cocaine. 95%

pure coca alkaloid, fresh from Bolivia and Columbia. And more safes brimming with Brown Gun Powder Afghani Heroin, Mexican Black Tar Heroin, Snow White Heroin from Thailand and pure Fentanyl from a direct source in Peking, China. You'd have on hand an entire United Nations contingency of dope. And then, you could have a staff of dope cookers, all vying to concoct, "the world's greatest crack rock" or "the galaxies most perfect speedball."

There could be another team of chemists cooking up every drug listed in, *"The Physician's Desk Reference."* And then for safety you could have a staff of brilliant physicians on hand who'd ensure your resurrection in case of any pesky overdose instances.

With more money than a hundred men could spend in a lifetime at his disposal, this passionless, incredibly wealthy, incredibly lost soul, was busted driving erratically after scoring thirty dollars' worth of crack cocaine.

He had nothing, no master plan of addiction, directing minions to do the ancillary dirty work. He had wealth without a shred of passion.

All he really had was a vile puddle of piss of an addiction that could not be quenched, and he also had a dead wife at home. She OD'd two weeks prior and was now idling away her days rotting in the second bath, her body morphing into an emulsified slurry of lost hope and dreams while her husband scored a few hits of crack on the street.

The whole rambling point of this sad saps story is this: Passion is necessary in one's life, without it you will eventually fall apart –regardless of position, status or wealth.

At the end of the day, what passion means to me is simply this: rejoicing in a pursuit which evokes great personal joy while positively contributing to the world. And I will die with the absolute confirmation; I was in this world to write.

Selling books is another matter entirely. Apples and oranges. While writing is and will forever remain a deep passion of mine, another is music. Around the time I began writing seriously, I picked up a guitar and told myself I was going to learn to play.

You're never too old... Yes you are.

Years back when I was about 11-12 years old, I had interest in the guitar and even saved up enough money to order one out of the Sears Catalog.

What I had in purchasing power I was lacking when it came to the patience required to learn how to play. Eventually not too long after my musical acquisition I hung it up.

It continued to remain in the back of my brain, my desire to play the guitar, but decade after decade I neglected to make another attempt of learning.

Once, while feeling rather artistic, I saw and bought: a guitar, tuner and learning guide packaged "learn to play rock-n-roll!" set at my local big box retailer. I returned the box set shortly thereafter once my liquid courage diminished.

Another decade or two later, at age 49, I decided to really, whole heartedly give learning to play one more time. I made the bold proclamation that I was not too old to learn how to play the guitar and my wonderful wife took note.

The following Christmas I opened a peculiar shaped, odd looking package to find my better half was going to make me put my money where my mouth was and so I did. She bought me a wonderful, inexpensive beginners' guitar (in fact it was a toy for children, and it made me laugh) that spurred me on to really challenge myself to learning. We picked out a different guitar after returning the toy, and I've been playing since.

The one biggest point to consider when deciding to do such things as learning to play guitar when you are older in life, is, well, you are older on in life.

Continuing with my guitar example let me detail how my peppiest steppin' enthusiasm in learning to play, was dampened by my age. It is never too late to learn but know you will have limitations due to your time spent on earth. The longer you wait to do anything the greater the negative effect gravity will have. This is easily notable in nature.

I'm right-handed so of course I strum with my right hand and I use my left hand to move up and down the fretboard. I'm normally rocking back and forth as I play as well as I rock my noggin out more often than not.

Take this physical action into consideration as I mention some of the surgical repairs I've had: two lower spine surgeries, right elbow tendon repaired, left shoulder two surgical repairs and now my upper spine is causing me problems and pain.

Nearly every key joint I use in playing guitar has had a repair or is painfully failing. I love to play and in the past six years I've gotten to where I sound good, but my playing time is limited due to my deteriorating musculoskeletal system.

At best I can play a half hour before my painful body reminds me of my age and I need to put the guitar down. It's very easy to see why learning to play is best left to fourteen-year-old Rock Gods in the making.

The take-away on this is simple: it may never be too late to do something however time does take a toll on us. All of us. So, do what you want to do sooner than later because your heart and ambition may be ready to go 100% but your body may reject any ideas involving moving against gravity altogether.

The only thing more difficult than pursuing passion later in life, such as my guitar/arthritis example, is getting cut down completely by death, just when you weren't looking.

***

When I was nineteen, I was with my best friend, Merrick, from high school when he died in my arms after a horrific motorcycle accident. That wasn't the bad part.

No, going to his mom's house that evening, prepared to console and mourn with her and his brothers, was a real, "gotcha ya," moment in my life.

That early evening, several hours after the accident, I sheepishly made my way, uneased by the dramatic, life changing events of the day, to Merrick's sweet mom's. Of the five guys I went to high school with and hung around with after school, Merrick's mom was the coolest, kindest, most genuine mom of all.

"Hi Lucky, where's Merrick," she beamed while opening the door to invite me in. I felt a massive blow to my gut as I realized I was going to be the one to tell her baby boy was dead. He was gone at 19, not even a full year out of high school.

Nearly forty years later I think of him more than anyone I've ever met in my life. He is with me daily. The poor kid never had a chance to really live, to really spread his wings. Often in life since his demise, I've felt I had to take two servings of –everything.

One for me and one for him. This doctrine of which I've self-prescribed I've found to be unsound, and sometimes bad. I'll not stop, I know it may shorten my life, but I feel I must do it, not only for me, but for Merrick too.

You might imagine I'm not a big believer in bucket lists, I'm not. Bucket lists are for losers, action today is for winners. I understand loss and pain are universal, yet at the same time positively unique for us all. We all agree less pain (physical/emotional) is better. So don't induce pain caused by waiting to long to… Do what you feel passion for; live your dream sooner than later.

***

Years ago, I read a biography of Thomas Alva Edison, one of America's most brilliant minds and prolific passionate inventor. Afterward one point always stuck with me.

Early on in his career he found himself spending a great deal of time inventing simple little contraptions that were quirky and interesting but had no real practical use or general interest. He determined he was going to need to put his passion to use and invent something people were interested in.

In no time at all, thanks to electricity, people were toasting bread on countertops, listening to recorded music and there was an explosion of people getting busy in the bedroom with lights on for the very first time. Indubitably, good times were being had by all thanks to Edison's passion.

I think we are all most alive when we challenge ourselves. I also think we are all most joyous when we know, definitively know deep within, we squeezed every ounce of ourselves, into our passion project.

I believe this is what motivated Thomas A, that maybe he felt unless his passion was used for the greatest good, it was mere folly. Not so much that he wanted to be mega-wealthy, but he wanted to do the greatest good.

When I decided to live the life I've always dreamed of, I immediately quit my job in corporate America and began writing poetry. With my last reserve of immaturity, I flipped off corporate America by sending an F-bomb laden, "you guys are all screwed up and I'm leaving," letter, to all email I had available: team internal, corporate general, customers, distributors, partner teams. I blew it all up, directing a vicious scorched earth policy on my former career as a software development engineer.

I was compelled to depart under such childish circumstances because I did not want a bridge available to go back on. I wanted to destroy any possibility of going back to the ease and comfort of my old career, my passionless life. I accepted the fact that I am on this Earth to write, so BAM, I made it so.

That and the fact my last employer, a little software and gaming console company in Redmond, Washington that starts with an, "M," had some serious pull in the industry. Nobody was gonna hire me after that.

And that was my plan; go all in, go big or go home, to put up or shut up and any other snappy, motivating quips to keep me on the path. Now, this is where the investing of capitol comes back into play.

Find Your Passion in Life

I think a great way to find passion is to begin by doing volunteer or charity work. If you begin altruistic endeavors without expectations or apply yourself in an area that you have no expertise, maybe you'll find a new spark you never knew you existed.

Maybe you'll throw a 55-gallon drum of combustible obsession, downright explosive type stuff at the new spark in your life and kaboom! The next thing you know you have more than a new special interest or distraction; you may find a guaranteed slice of good ole passion.

Before I ever knew I was a fervent "dog person" I did volunteer work at a dog shelter. I took this up shortly after I left the Canadian telecom company. In-between cleaning kennels out I spent time walking many different dogs. To be honest, I actually began volunteering at the shelter because I was being a bit of a dog myself, having had followed an attractive single friend to the task.

I had time on my hands as ski season was ending, frolicking in the Cascades had consumed much of my waking time since receiving a respectable severance package from my previous big spending employer. These severance packages, and every other ridiculously over the top incentive or bonus, were excessive and were the bane of the company's existence.

I believe it was the offering of silky soft golden parachutes to the upper echelon executives as well as the favorable in any light packages handed down to me and the thousands of others like me, that finally caused the whole organization to implode.

These many zeroed gifts came back to bite everyone that gladly cashed the whoppers in that the company stock was still unavailable to cash out for a period, stock that was held in their retirement accounts. It was diving wildly until it finally reached a writhing death in the throes of a hundred happy attorneys.

***

If you're stuck, get a dog. And keep the dog through the most inopportune situations. Building a bond with another living being will open your eyes to a different dimension, call it love, acceptance trust.

If you're unable to give a puppy a proper home due to the constraints of apartment living, get a cat.

I don't want to offend anyone, there is no hierarchy for love. It either is or it isn't. Dog, cat, goldfish. It doesn't matter, it's all about the generation of love that which caring for, loving, an animal does for us sensitive human beings.

The unfriendliness, irritation and general overall disdain you may feel for the other seven and a half billion or so other inhabitants on the planet, will require your acceptance to be free. Give it time.

Until you meet up with and connect to your true passion in this life, fake it till you make it, so they say.

All joking aside, creating wealth is an empty endevor unless you have passion. I implore you to take a long hard look at yourself and find acceptance to resolve issues that have weighed you down in the past.

I believe this process is clearer and significantly easier and more insightful with age. In fact, I think if you are paying attention and are open to suggestions and creative input, your passions become clearer and quicker.

When I began writing full time, I was exceptionally critical and unsupportive about my abilities and creativity. This weighed heavily on me at times, but I got past it. Since then, I've come to a place of supreme self-confidence and acceptance of the world around me.

I mentioned earlier that we should be our own best advocate. My initial declaration was with respect to our financial situation however this proclamation is appropriate in every facet of life.

Deploy it and you will reap tremendous reward. Absolutely nobody knows you as completely, honestly and truthfully, as you. Work with your assets as well as your deficits. Embrace both. Understand both, love both –live.

Accept your deficits. We all can't do everything. In your career, your relationships, your creative endeavors and even in your hobbies exercise your known strengths, recognize your weaknesses.

I love playing basketball but I'm too short to ever dunk so I stick to perfecting free throws. In business I did not have interest nor patience in managing a staff, so I stayed the course of executive sales and engineering.

I believe the more you understand and accept how you operate, the stronger you will be in any enterprise.

I think most people operating in the world today are reluctant to acknowledge themselves completely. Sweeping away nasty, persistent personal proclivities seems to be a national pastime.

My Uncle Tim was a man that seemed to never have a care in the world. His pizzazz and flash were intoxicating to the eleven-year-old me. I wanted what he had. The gorgeous mansion, a brand-new top of the line Mercedes Benz every year, extended vacations to tropical destinations and more than anything, I wanted his kind of style. He continued to exude stellar confidence and project limitless knowledge until his world imploded.

It was several years after our last fishing trip to Southern Illinois, my folks had gotten wise and relocated the family to the Pacific Northwest, when I began to hear of cracks in his foundation. It started when he was due to buy the current year new Mercedes. Instead of the new Benz, he drove home in a three-year-old Cadillac.

This simple act screamed of gloom and doom. Over the course of a single summer my brilliant, endearing Uncle Tim lost his seat on the Mercantile Exchange, saw his house go into foreclosure and lastly, left Chicago for Northern Wisconsin where he had a mistress and twin seven-year-old boys. The person I idolized for my entire childhood was found to be an illusion, nothing more than smoke and mirrors.

For all the money he seemed to make, Uncle Tim never had a pot to potty in. And after all the life lessons on honesty and hard work he professed, I was dismayed to realize he was a broke, dishonest, lying dead beat. When the dust settled it came to light that the man was lecherous to a formidable degree. Repulsive to the core.

When he could no longer keep up with the illusion of himself that he created, he simply skipped town with his tail between his legs and debt that went into the millions. It wasn't only banks and financial institutions he owed money to, he left every single friend he had in the windy city with a bogus IOU.

***

Childhood romances are sometimes negated by the wisdom we gain with age. Looking back, I appreciate what we had, my Uncle Tim and I, when I was a kid, no doubt we had a blast together.

That fact won't change however my understanding of the man, my opinion of him now, as a 53-year-old adult, is I can only imagine he is a lonely old man who will likely die without ever experiencing passion, joy, connection to others or understanding the satisfaction one finds in contributing to humanity.

Once again, be your own best advocate. The people you look up to may be other than what they report. Companies agendas change, lovers' feelings change, best friends forever change. Your socks and underwear change, for everyone's benefit hopefully they're changed frequently.

There's no need to want to one-up me on my reported, "summer of stink." The funk I fashioned and nonchalantly sported as a trademarked imperceptible uniform in 2005 is best left as it stands: mephitic lore of legendary proportion. Leave it alone unless you are ready to unabashedly dive in full-throttle, the deep end of commitment and I'm talkin' no baby wipes either. Baby!

The only one absolute single continuum in our lives that is pervasive and entrenched in us all, is we are the only ones that are with us for our entire lives. Sure, people know us but who knows us completely?

Everyone that knows us know us as much as we will allow them to know. Know what I'm saying.

Once we're shot out of mommy's birth canal, after being with onboard with her 24x7 for our entire newbie lives up until that point, we eventually have alone time.

Question everything, satisfy your curiosity and be true to you. Don't believe anyone's B.S. Be true to you, that includes calling yourself out on your own bullshit, as best you/we can.

***

After all my insistence of reporting one should never believe in another's guarantees or promises and professing one should never take a "hot stock tip," at face value and you must always, always exercise due diligence before making any investment decisions, It seems that works for most all-important matters in life as well. But forget all that for a quick second, I've got a hot guarantee that's unbeatable. If I used emojis you'd see a grinning little guy right here.

And it's not even so much financial advice that it is a thought, universal conjecture, hearsay if you will. Come to understand yourself, spend time alone to search your soul identifying what you deeply feel connected to, what you need in your life to satiate your audacious need for passion and you will find joy, bliss and contentment with the world. That is a promise. Wink.

Self-centric vs Self-ish

One last mention that's not advise so much as it is an observation or acknowledgment of universal human bad behavior. People will disappoint us; on this I will bet the farm every time. But give people a break, it's only a matter of time we all need a break ourselves.

When it comes to people look for similarities, differences are too easy. Continually test yourself in all facets of life, mentally catalog your life experiences for reference in the future. All experiences, good and bad, are opportunities and assistance in defining ourselves.

Know yourself, accept and love yourself. Do these things and wealth, along with everything else good in life will fall into place.

Giving you a great stock tip to end this book would be much too easy, having faith in you, every single one of you, faith that you can do anything you put your mind to, this is what I give you as a guaranteed promise. One with unbelievable returns.

Do these things and when you reach the zenith of your potential, when you are living the life of your dreams you will not only benefit yourself, inherently you will benefit others.

I sincerely believe any human being's maximum potential by nature includes positively contributing to the world around them. Do these things and the world is all yours. Berkshire Hathaway will seem like child's play.

***

There's one more last point I want to make about finding passion in your life. In terms of having a financial security blanket, expand your passionate horizons because money can be as easy as creating a product or using one of your passionate interests. I'll go back to my guitar example.

I mentioned how playing music helped me become a better writer, helped me gain confidence in my other artistic pursuits because I could easily discern when I play a good note or a bad note. I can always tell.

I continually reassured myself that if I could learn to play Bob Marley's "Redemption Song," I could do just about anything. So, after practicing religiously I wanted to truly test myself. I took my guitar to the park by my house, sat on a bench with my guitar case opened at my feet and I began to play Rastafarian Gospel.

Never before has a man smiled as wide over forty-two cents as I did when a passing stroller smiled, nodded at me then tossed a quarter, three nickels and two pennies into my case.

It never ceases to positively amaze me to my every fiber, just when I think I have this thing called life all figured out I get thunderstruck by more glory. It's true.

That forty-two cents was the universe not only telling me I was on the correct path in my life, words, music, art, color, creation but that I can get paid for doin' it too!

I immediately went home reveling in the jingling change in my pocket and added to my Renascence Man Resume: Professional Guitar Player. In case for some reason I am no longer able to write stories and I go broke, I'll go play my guitar.

I earnestly hope I do not disappoint any readers when they come to find, after all is said and done, this financial wizard is entirely satisfied, eager for not another cent, after a daily return of a few pieces of loose change.

Today in life I don't want "extra," I just need enough and any excess I'll gladly share.

George Bailey isn't the only richest man in town and there's plenty of room for more so join. Merry Christmas.

-The End-

www.ingramcontent.com/pod-product-compliance
Lightning Source LLC
Chambersburg PA
CBHW030952240526
45463CB00016B/2501